INSIDE THE NFL

WASHINGTON COMMANDERS

by Will Graves

Abdo & Daughters
MIDDLE GRADE NONFICTION

An imprint of Abdo Publishing
abdobooks.com

ABDOBOOKS.COM

Published by Abdo Publishing, a division of ABDO, PO Box 398166, Minneapolis, Minnesota 55439.

Printed in China.
052025
092025

THIS BOOK CONTAINS RECYCLED MATERIALS

Cover Photos: G. Fiume/Getty Images Sport/Getty Images (Jayden Daniels); Focus on Sport/Getty Images Sport/Getty Images (Darrell Green)
Interior Photos: Cooper Neill/Getty Images Sport/Getty Images, 4–5, 63; Dylan Buell/Getty Images Sport/Getty Images, 6, 10; Andy Lyons/Getty Images Sport/Getty Images, 7; John Smolek/Icon Sportswire/Getty Images, 9; Alika Jenner/Getty Images Sport/Getty Images, 11, 61 (bottom right); Abdo Publishing, 12–13, 58; AP Images, 14–15, 17, 18, 19, 24–25; Bettmann/Getty Images, 16, 21, 30; Mitchell Layton/Getty Images Sport/Getty Images, 20, 60 (bottom); Focus on Sport/Getty Images, 22; Focus on Sport/Getty Images Sport/Getty Images, 23, 36–37, 41, 43, 60 (top); Paul Spinelli/AP Images, 26, 44, 61 (top left); John Iacono/Sports Illustrated/Getty Images, 27; Owen C. Shaw/Getty Images Sport/Getty Images, 28; Ronald C. Modra/Sports Illustrated/Getty Images, 29; Nate Fine/Getty Images Sport/Getty Images, 31; Elise Amendola/AP Images, 32, 61 (bottom left); Al Messerschmidt Archive/AP Images, 34, 39; George Rose/Getty Images Sport/Getty Images, 35; Mark Duncan/AP Images, 38; Paul Spinelli/NFL Photos/AP Images, 40; Ezra O. Shaw/Allsport/Getty Images Sport/Getty Images, 45; G. Newman Lowrance/AP Images, 46, 56; Jamie Squire/Getty Images Sport/Getty Images, 47; Nick Wass/AP Images, 48–49; L. M. Otero/AP Images, 50; Evan Vucci/AP Images, 51; John Froschauer/AP Images, 52; Rob Carr/Getty Images Sport/Getty Images, 53; Richard Lipski/AP Images, 55; Lee Coleman/Icon Sportswire/Getty Images, 57, 61 (top right); Patrick Smith/Getty Images Sport/Getty Images, 59

Editor: Chrös McDougall
Series Designer: Laura Graphenteen
Production Designer: Ryan Gale

Library of Congress Control Number: 2024948476

Publisher's Cataloging-in-Publication Data

Names: Graves, Will, author.
Title: Washington Commanders / by Will Graves
Description: Minneapolis, Minnesota: Abdo Publishing, 2026 | Series: Inside the NFL | Includes online resources and index.
Identifiers: ISBN 9781098296933 (lib. bdg.) | ISBN 9798384919452 (ebook)
Subjects: LCSH: Washington Commanders (Football team)--Juvenile literature. | National Football League--Juvenile literature. | Football teams--Juvenile literature. | American football--Juvenile literature.
Classification: DDC 796.333--dc23

CONTENTS

Washington Commanders fans had high hopes for rookie quarterback Jayden Daniels heading into the 2024 season.

CHAPTER 1

THE ANSWER

The Washington Commanders faced an early test in the 2024 National Football League (NFL) season. After a 1–1 start, the Commanders hit the road to take on the 0–2 Cincinnati Bengals in Week 3. Despite having the better record, Washington wasn't favored. Many thought the talented Bengals would cruise to victory.

Washington has a rich history that includes five league championships. But for much of the 2000s, the Commanders found themselves looking up in the standings. The team seemed to cycle through quarterbacks while posting just four winning seasons and one playoff berth over the previous 24 seasons. So when the Bengals took an early lead on a 41-yard touchdown, an easy win appeared on the way. But this wasn't the same Washington team.

The Commanders had selected quarterback Jayden Daniels second overall in that spring's NFL Draft. And in front of the national *Monday Night Football* audience, he was about to show why.

Commanders running back Brian Robinson marches into the end zone against the Cincinnati Bengals in 2024.

On Washington's first drive, Daniels connected with Luke McCaffrey for a 30-yard gain on fourth down. Four plays later, running back Brian Robinson scored on a 1-yard run to tie the game.

Washington's second drive looked a lot like its first. Daniels found Noah Brown for a 16-yard gain. Daniels then flipped a pass to McCaffrey for 11 yards before running back Austin Ekeler burst through the defense for a 24-yard score that gave Washington a 14–7 lead.

Bengals quarterback Joe Burrow had started strong, too. And he responded by leading his team to a field goal. But the Cincinnati defense couldn't seem to find a way to slow Washington down.

Washington wide receiver Terry McLaurin hauls in a 55-yard catch against the Bengals.

The 6-foot-4 Daniels could beat defenses with his strong passing arm, or he could burst past them on a run. Washington's third drive turned into a showcase for Daniels's unique talents. He launched a 55-yard bomb to streaking wide receiver Terry McLaurin. On the next play, Daniels faked a handoff and kept the ball himself. He moved to his left and easily walked into the end zone for a 4-yard touchdown that helped Washington build a 21–13 halftime lead. Something special was brewing.

A FINISHING TOUCH

Burrow had arrived in the NFL with great fanfare. The quarterback nicknamed "Joe Cool" won the 2019 Heisman Trophy as college football's best player. His passing led the high-powered Louisiana State University (LSU) Tigers to that year's national title. The NFL's top draft pick the following spring, Burrow lifted the Bengals to a Super Bowl appearance in his second season.

Washington fans were hoping for a similar trajectory for Daniels. He had gotten off to a good start by winning the Heisman Trophy while playing for LSU in 2023. And on a cool September night in downtown Cincinnati, Daniels offered a hint that he might not just meet expectations but exceed them.

The biggest test came in the final minutes. With Washington holding a 31–26 lead, the Commanders faced third-and-seven from the Cincinnati 27. The safe play would have been to run the ball to burn some time off the clock before kicking a field goal. That would have given Washington an eight-point lead with only two minutes remaining. The Commanders weren't thinking about playing it safe, though.

While watching film to prepare for the game, McLaurin had keyed in on a potential Bengals weakness. If the opportunity arose, he thought he could beat his defender on a deep pass. Commanders offensive coordinator Kliff Kingsbury thought it was worth the gamble.

McLaurin lined up wide to Daniels's right. He took off at the snap and ran as fast as he could toward the goal line. Cincinnati blitzed, and Daniels quickly saw a Bengals defender right in his face.

NO WAY

Jayden Daniels's breakout success had a strange side effect on Washington punter Tress Way. The two-time Pro Bowl selection didn't punt at all during Washington's back-to-back wins over the New York Giants and Cincinnati Bengals. That's because Washington either scored or took a knee to run out the clock at the end of every possession. Way was still busy with his side job as the holder for Commanders kicker Austin Seibert.

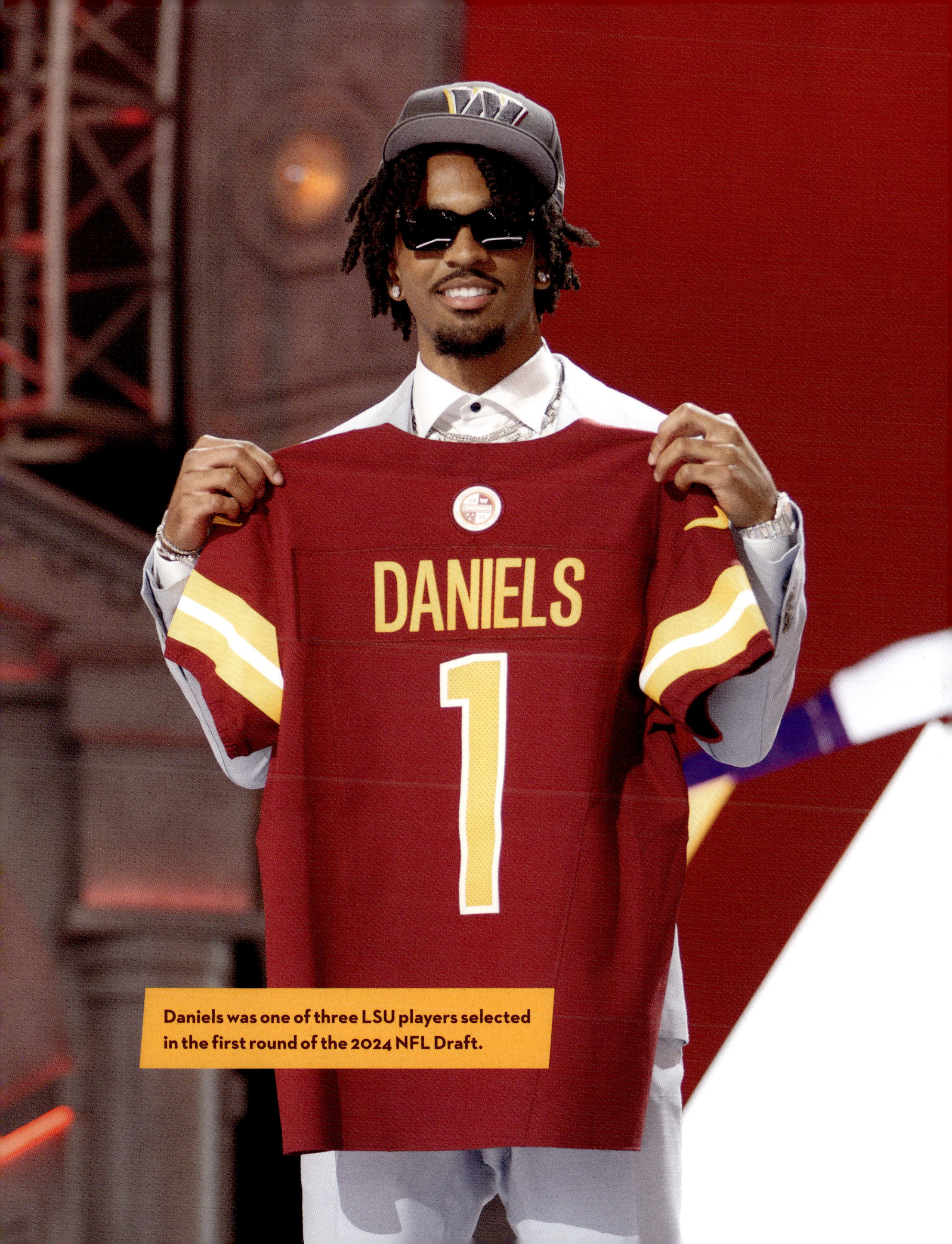

Daniels was one of three LSU players selected in the first round of the 2024 NFL Draft.

McLaurin's fourth-quarter touchdown catch put Washington up 38–26 with just 2:10 to play against the Bengals.

It turned out to be no big deal. Daniels uncorked a high, arching throw that settled into McLaurin's hands just inside the orange-and-black-painted end zone. Daniels's second touchdown pass of the day gave the Commanders a 38–26 lead that even Joe Cool couldn't overcome.

Ultimately completing 21 of his 23 passes, Daniels's 91.3 completion percentage was the highest in NFL history for a rookie. But most importantly, Washington held on for a 38–33 victory that did more than push the team's record to 2–1. It gave a long-overdue dose of hope to a team that had spent most of the previous 30 years as an afterthought. The Jayden Daniels era had officially arrived.

"I put in the work," Daniels said. "What's done in the dark will always come to light. I just know that I prepare for these moments week in and week out. I just have to go out there and play football and execute."

"I PUT IN THE WORK. WHAT'S DONE IN THE DARK WILL ALWAYS COME TO LIGHT. I JUST KNOW THAT I PREPARE FOR THESE MOMENTS WEEK IN AND WEEK OUT. I JUST HAVE TO GO OUT THERE AND PLAY FOOTBALL AND EXECUTE."

—JAYDEN DANIELS

Daniels's breakout performance against the Bengals showed that he could be an elite NFL quarterback.

NFL TEAMS MAP

NFC

NFC EAST

- DALLAS COWBOYS
- NEW YORK GIANTS
- PHILADELPHIA EAGLES
- WASHINGTON COMMANDERS

NFC WEST

- ARIZONA CARDINALS
- LOS ANGELES RAMS
- SAN FRANCISCO 49ERS
- SEATTLE SEAHAWKS

NFC NORTH

- CHICAGO BEARS
- DETROIT LIONS
- GREEN BAY PACKERS
- MINNESOTA VIKINGS

NFC SOUTH

- ATLANTA FALCONS
- CAROLINA PANTHERS
- NEW ORLEANS SAINTS
- TAMPA BAY BUCCANEERS

AFC

AFC EAST

- BUFFALO BILLS
- MIAMI DOLPHINS
- NEW ENGLAND PATRIOTS
- NEW YORK JETS

AFC WEST

- DENVER BRONCOS
- KANSAS CITY CHIEFS
- LAS VEGAS RAIDERS
- LOS ANGELES CHARGERS

AFC NORTH

- BALTIMORE RAVENS
- CINCINNATI BENGALS
- CLEVELAND BROWNS
- PITTSBURGH STEELERS

AFC SOUTH

- HOUSTON TEXANS
- INDIANAPOLIS COLTS
- JACKSONVILLE JAGUARS
- TENNESSEE TITANS

George Preston Marshall helped found the Commanders franchise in 1932 and owned the team for 37 years.

CHAPTER 2

CAPITAL GAINS

THE COMMANDERS' STORY BEGAN MORE THAN 400 MILES (644 KM) north of the nation's capital. In 1932, George Preston Marshall was part of a group that founded a team known as the Boston Braves. The team got off to a solid start, going 4–4–2 in its first season. However, its success off the field was a different story. The Braves lost $46,000. That was a fortune in the middle of the Great Depression, a period of financial hardship in the United States. The team's other three owners dropped out, leaving Marshall in charge.

Before the 1933 season, the team moved to a new stadium. Marshall also changed its name to the Boston Redskins. The name was likely meant to highlight the team's Native American ties, though the term *redskin* was often used as a slur and remained controversial for years to come.

Boston and the Green Bay Packers, *with ball*, met for the 1936 NFL championship.

The team showed improvement in the coming seasons and ultimately reached the 1936 NFL Championship Game. However, the Green Bay Packers trounced Boston 21–6. Meanwhile, Marshall had grown frustrated by the lack of fan support from the city, so ahead of the 1937 season, he moved the team to Washington, DC.

ON THE MOVE

When the NFL began play in 1920, it had 14 teams based mostly in the Midwest. By 1937, the league had settled to 10 teams, all based in the Midwest or Northeast. In making its move, Washington became the NFL's first team south of the Mason-Dixon line that divided the country's North and South.

The team arrived at its new home with a new star in tow. Washington selected Texas Christian quarterback Sammy Baugh with the sixth pick in the 1937 draft. The player known as "Slingin' Sammy" helped change the way football was played. When he came into the league, teams relied heavily on running the ball. Passing was considered too dangerous, especially when a team was deep in its own territory.

Baugh's strong right arm ushered in a new passing era in the NFL. He led the league in passing yards during his rookie season while leading Washington back to the championship game. Facing the mighty Chicago Bears at their Wrigley Field home, Baugh threw for 335 yards and three touchdowns. Washington won 28–21 and celebrated its first season in its new home with an NFL championship.

Baugh wasn't just a talented passer. He was one of the most versatile players of his generation. Like many NFL players at the time, Baugh played multiple positions. In addition to starring at quarterback, he played safety on defense and became one of the most effective punters in NFL history. In 1943, Baugh led the league in passing yards, interceptions, and punting average.

Quarterback Sammy Baugh joined the team in 1937, the same year it arrived in Washington.

Baugh won an NFL-record six passing titles during his career.

PUTTING ON A SHOW

Fans who came out to Washington's Griffith Stadium to watch Baugh and the rest of the team weren't just treated to lots of wins. They also enjoyed the sounds of the team's official marching band. Launched in 1938, the band was the first of its kind in the NFL and remains active today. Marshall also introduced halftime shows and made sure fans who couldn't make it to the game could follow the team by establishing a radio network that broadcast Washington games throughout the South.

Washington was one of the NFL's most successful teams during Baugh's career, though the club didn't always come out on top. No team had a better record than Washington's 9–2 in 1940. After a win against the Bears, Marshall taunted the opponents. The Bears responded by running up the score in the NFL title game.

Chicago scored 11 touchdowns in a 73–0 demolition. It remains the most lopsided defeat in NFL history. There were no nets behind the goalposts in those days, so the Bears kept kicking their extra points into the stands. It got so bad officials asked the Bears to stop kicking. Chicago agreed, opting to run in its extra points instead.

Washington earned a measure of revenge two years later, beating the Bears 14–6 to claim its second league title. Baugh retired after the 1952 season. Eleven years later, in 1963, he was part of the first class inducted into the Pro Football Hall of Fame.

Hall of Fame receiver Bobby Mitchell led the NFL in receiving yards in 1962 and 1963.

Baugh's departure led to lean times for the team. Washington was among the worst teams in the NFL during the 1950s and 1960s. The team's troubles extended beyond the field. Washington, DC, agreed to build a new stadium for the team in the city's southeast area in the early 1960s. But the US Secretary of the Interior at the time told Marshall the stadium might not be available to the team if Marshall did not integrate the roster. At the time, Washington was the only club in the NFL that had never had a Black player.

Marshall planned to fight the government but eventually gave in. Washington traded for Cleveland Browns receiver Bobby Mitchell and running back Leroy Jackson in December 1961. With that, they became the first Black players in club history.

SONNY DAYS

Washington's fortunes began to turn in the late 1960s. The team traded for quarterback Sonny Jurgensen in 1964. He teamed up with Mitchell and wide receiver Charley Taylor to make Washington's offense one of the most exciting in the NFL. On November 27, 1966, Washington beat the New York Giants 72–41. It's still the highest-scoring game in NFL history.

The strong-armed Jurgensen led the NFL in passing three times in his first six seasons in Washington. Still, the team had trouble climbing into contention. That seemed to be changing when Washington brought in Vince Lombardi. The legendary coach had guided

ROCKIN' RFK

Washington's rise in the 1970s made Robert F. Kennedy (RFK) Memorial Stadium the place to be every fall in the nation's capital. Named DC Stadium when it opened in 1961, it was renamed in honor of former US Attorney General Robert F. Kennedy in 1969. Washington sold out every game at RFK Stadium from 1967 through 1996, when the team moved to a new home in nearby Maryland.

Washington fullback A. D. Whitfield runs for the first of his three touchdowns against the New York Giants in their November 1966 game.

the Green Bay Packers to five championships between the 1961 and 1967 seasons. After giving up his coaching duties in 1968, Lombardi sought a return to the sideline and moved to Washington in 1969. It did not take long for the much-respected Lombardi to work his magic. Washington finished 7–5–2 in 1969, good enough for second place in the Capitol Division.

Unfortunately, Lombardi's time in Washington was short. On June 24, 1970, the Hall of Fame coach checked into a hospital because he wasn't feeling well. He was diagnosed with cancer and died just over two months later at age 57.

THE OVER THE HILL GANG

Washington brought in George Allen as head coach in 1971. The former Los Angeles Rams coach had a reputation for turning losing teams into winning ones behind his motto "The Future is Now." Allen had a specific plan on how to build a team: he would trade away draft picks for veteran players with more experience.

The plan worked to near perfection in Washington. Allen began acquiring stars nearing the end of their careers, promising them playing time and a chance to win. By 1972, Washington had the right mix of young and old players, such as 25-year-old running back Larry Brown and 36-year-old linebacker Jack Pardee. The team won 10 of its first 11 games on its way to an 11–3 record and the National Football Conference (NFC) East division title. After winning two playoff games, including against the defending Super Bowl–champion Dallas Cowboys, Washington was headed to its first Super Bowl.

Washington running back Larry Brown led the NFL in total yards and was named Most Valuable Player (MVP) in 1972.

The Miami Dolphins awaited. Behind their

The Miami Dolphins and their "No-Name Defense" shut down quarterback Billy Kilmer and Washington in Super Bowl VII on January 14, 1973.

"No-Name Defense," the Dolphins became the first team to reach the Super Bowl unbeaten. Washington had trouble moving the ball all game, and Dolphins safety Jake Scott intercepted quarterback Billy Kilmer twice. Washington's brightest moment came late in the game when Miami attempted a field goal. Washington blocked Garo Yepremian's kick. The ball bounced back to Yepremian, who fumbled trying to throw a pass. Washington's Mike Bass grabbed the ball and raced 49 yards for a touchdown to cut Miami's lead to 14–7. However, Washington would get no closer, and the Dolphins finished the season a perfect 17–0.

Allen kept Washington competitive throughout the 1970s, but eventually "the Over the Hill Gang" got too old. Allen was fired after the 1977 season. His replacement, former star Pardee, lasted only three seasons, failing to make the playoffs in any of them. However, brighter days were coming to the nation's capital.

Powerful running back John Riggins helped turn Washington into a power during the early 1980s.

CHAPTER 3

AWESOME EIGHTIES

JOE GIBBS EARNED A REPUTATION AS ONE OF THE TOP OFFENSIVE MINDS in the NFL while calling the plays for the San Diego Chargers. Jack Kent Cooke, Washington's owner since 1969, thought Gibbs could deliver a Super Bowl title. So in 1981, the team hired Gibbs as head coach. He and general manager Bobby Beathard believed the foundation was in place for Washington to turn things around quickly.

The foundation received a boost not long after Gibbs took over when powerful running back John Riggins returned to the team. Nicknamed "the Diesel," the rugged, colorful Riggins had sat out the 1980 season while in a contract dispute with the club. When he returned to Washington in June 1981, he told his teammates, "I'm bored, I'm broke, and I'm back."

"I'M BORED, I'M BROKE, AND I'M BACK."

—JOHN RIGGINS

Riggins gave Gibbs an engine in the backfield he could build an offense around. The next step of Gibbs's plan was building a line for Riggins to run behind. He found one in a group that assistant coach Joe Bugel called "the Hogs." Led by guard Russ Grimm and center Jeff Bostic, the Hogs were known for their size and their ability to create huge running lanes for Riggins to barrel through.

Joe Theismann took over as Washington's full-time starting quarterback in 1978.

Quarterback Joe Theismann directed a passing attack that included a group of undersized receivers, including 5-foot-7-inch Alvin Garrett and 5-foot-8-inch Virgil Seay. Theismann called the group "the Smurfs" after a popular children's cartoon show about a group of small blue elves. When the Smurfs reached the end zone, they became "the Fun Bunch." Whenever one of the wide receivers or tight ends caught a touchdown pass, they gathered in the end zone and leaped in the air at the same time, exchanging high fives along the way.

"The Fun Bunch" celebrates a Washington touchdown.

A SUPER RUN

Washington finished the 1981 season strong to end 8–8, and then it opened 1982 with a pair of victories. However, the season took a turn when the NFL players went on strike. They refused to play for 57 days while in a labor dispute with league owners.

When the players came back, Washington rolled to an 8–1 record in the shortened regular season before breezing through its first two playoff games. Only the Dallas Cowboys stood in the way of a trip to the Super Bowl.

In 1982, Washington kicker Mark Moseley became the first kicker in NFL history to win the league's MVP Award.

The rivalry between Washington and Dallas began in the 1960s but reached new heights in the 1970s, when the Cowboys often got the best of Washington on their way to two Super Bowl wins. Dallas had also been the only team to beat Washington in 1982. Ahead of the playoff showdown, fans in RFK Stadium

Riggins runs 43 yards for a touchdown against the Miami Dolphins in Super Bowl XVII after the 1982 season.

chanted "We Want Dallas!" They got their wish, and their team got revenge with a 31–17 win.

"This is our Super Bowl. This was everything rolled into one," Gibbs said. "[Washington] versus Dallas, the team we wanted to beat the most. How can you top that?"

"[WASHINGTON] VERSUS DALLAS, THE TEAM WE WANTED TO BEAT THE MOST. HOW CAN YOU TOP THAT?"

—JOE GIBBS

The actual Super Bowl was a rematch from a decade earlier with the Miami Dolphins. Trailing 17–13 midway through the fourth quarter, Washington had the ball facing fourth-and-one at the Miami 43. That's when the Diesel got rolling. Theismann turned and handed the ball off to Riggins on a play called "70 chip." Riggins broke through an attempted tackle and raced to the end zone in one of the most famous runs in Super Bowl history. Behind the running back's Super Bowl–record 166 rushing yards, Washington won 27–17 to claim the city's first NFL championship in 40 years.

Theismann (7) and Washington fell short against the Los Angeles Raiders in Super Bowl XVIII on January 22, 1984.

SETBACKS AND COMEBACKS

Washington seemed poised to reign over the NFL again in 1983. The team set an NFL record for points scored in a season, racking up 541 while going 14–2. Riggins set a new single-season mark by scoring 24 touchdowns, while Theismann earned the league's MVP honors after throwing for 29 scores. Only a pair of one-point losses, both on *Monday Night Football*, kept Washington from finishing with a perfect 16–0 record.

Two playoff wins sent Washington back to the Super Bowl, this time to face the Los Angeles Raiders. The teams had met at RFK Stadium earlier in the season, with Washington rallying for a thrilling 37–35 win. However, the Raiders proved much tougher the second time around, shutting down Washington's offense in a dominant 38–9 victory.

Washington returned to the playoffs in 1984 but fell in the divisional round. Time started to catch up to the 36-year-old Theismann in 1985. By the time Washington hosted the New York Giants on *Monday Night Football* that November, he had only eight touchdowns compared to 16 interceptions. Early in the second quarter, Theismann dropped back to pass when three Giants swarmed him for a sack, breaking Theismann's right leg in the process. He was rushed to the hospital for emergency surgery. While he made a full recovery, Theismann never played again.

Medical personnel care for Theismann after his gruesome injury against the New York Giants in 1985.

Washington quarterback Doug Williams played in only five regular-season games in 1987.

GOING FOR IT

Gibbs had two options to replace Theismann in 1986. One was 1984 third-round pick Jay Schroeder. The other was veteran Doug Williams, who had joined the team before the season. Williams expected to be the starter. Instead, he watched glumly from the bench as Schroeder set a new club record for passing yards while leading Washington to the NFC title game. However, the season ended there with a 17–0 loss to the rival Giants.

Before the 1987 season, the team was ready to trade Williams to the Oakland Raiders. The quarterback's bags were even packed for California. However, Gibbs had a change of heart. He told Williams,

"I got a gut feeling that somewhere along this season you are going to come in here and we are going to win this thing." Williams stayed.

STRIKING AGAIN

Washington began the 1987 season 1-1. Then the NFL players went on strike for the second time in five years. This time, when the regular NFL players held signs while walking picket lines to protest, the league brought in replacement players. When the strike ended after 24 days, Washington stood in first place at 4-1. It stayed there the rest of the regular season, even with Jay Schroeder and Doug Williams flip-flopping as the starting quarterback.

Gibbs's hunch proved correct. The coach needed both quarterbacks to piece together Washington's 11-4 season. Williams finally locked down the job in the final regular-season game by leading a 27-24 overtime comeback win over the Minnesota Vikings.

For the second straight year, Washington headed to Chicago to take on the Bears in the postseason. And for the second straight year, the visitors came out with the win. Williams threw for 207 yards with a touchdown, and speedy cornerback Darrell Green returned a punt 52 yards for a score. He memorably leaped over a Bears defender on his way to the end zone. Then a 17-10 win over the Vikings in the NFC Championship Game sent Washington to the Super Bowl for the third time in six years.

SECOND (QUARTER) TO NONE

For many years, there had been a misguided view in the NFL that Black quarterbacks could not win. Williams had shown throughout the playoffs that was not true. Then he became the first Black quarterback to start in a Super Bowl. However, opposing quarterback John Elway and the Denver Broncos struck first in

Super Bowl XXII and leaped to a 10–0 lead. Things got even worse for Washington when Williams twisted his knee while dropping back to pass and had to exit the game. However, Williams returned for the first play of the second quarter. What followed was maybe the most explosive performance in the history of football.

Starting with an 80-yard strike to Ricky Sanders, Washington buried the Broncos under an avalanche of touchdowns. Washington racked up 356 yards and five scores in the second quarter, with Williams throwing four touchdowns. And Washington did this while running just 18 plays from scrimmage. The team turned a 10-point deficit into a 35–10 lead by halftime.

Little-known Washington running back Timmy Smith runs 58 yards for a touchdown in the second quarter of Super Bowl XXII on January 31, 1988.

Washington's 35 points and 356 yards in the second quarter of Super Bowl XXII set playoff records for a single quarter.

Little-known running back Timmy Smith set a Super Bowl record by running for 204 yards, and he scored a pair of touchdowns. The day, however, belonged to Williams. He was named the game's MVP after finishing with 340 passing yards and four scores. And in doing so, he became the first Black quarterback to lead his team to a championship.

Even as players came and went, coach Joe Gibbs, *left*, was able to keep Washington among the NFL's best.

CHAPTER 4

TRIUMPH AND TRANSITION

NFL DYNASTIES ALMOST ALWAYS FEATURE A CONSISTENT GROUP OF core players, particularly at quarterback. In the 1970s, the Pittsburgh Steelers won four titles with Terry Bradshaw throwing passes. The San Francisco 49ers did the same in the 1980s behind Joe Montana. What Joe Gibbs built in Washington was different.

The first Super Bowl victory featured Joe Theismann under center. The second came on a magical night by Doug Williams. But Williams's run in Washington was short-lived due to health problems. By the spring of 1990, the hero of Washington's second Super Bowl title was no longer on the team.

A new era in Washington football was set to begin. Washington selected Mark Rypien out of Washington State with the 146th overall selection in the 1986 draft. Rypien endured some growing pains after taking over for an injured Williams in 1988 and 1989, but by 1990, he was firmly in control. The quarterback led Washington back to the playoffs and then to a win in the opening round. However, Washington fell 28–10 to the 49ers in the divisional round. Rypien threw three interceptions in the game.

Quarterback Mark Rypien was established as Washington's starter by the 1990s.

ALL ABOARD THE BANDWAGON

Rypien rebounded in a big way in 1991. He was the best quarterback in the NFL on the best team in the NFL. Over the course of five months, Gibbs and Washington put together one of the most dominant seasons ever.

The season started with a 45–0 blowout over the Detroit Lions, the largest margin of victory in team history. After the game, Gibbs said it was as good as Washington had ever played during his time in charge. It was also a sign of things to come. Washington rolled up one lopsided victory after another on its way to winning its first 11 games. Rypien led the NFL's highest-scoring offense behind the latest version of "the Hogs," who made sure their quarterback had

Left tackle Jim Lachey (79) and "the Hogs" gave Washington's offense plenty of time to create plays in 1991.

plenty of time to find receivers Art Monk, Gary Clark, and Ricky Sanders downfield.

The receivers called themselves "the Posse," and they spent 1991 piling up touchdown after touchdown. Clark and Monk both topped 1,000 receiving yards. Sanders added five touchdowns. Meanwhile, the running back trio of Earnest Byner, Ricky Ervins, and Gerald Riggs made teams pay if they spent too much time focusing on slowing down the Posse. Cornerback Darrell Green, still plenty fast at age 31, led a dominant defense.

There was a sense around the nation's capital as fall turned into winter that another championship was on the way. *Washington Post*

Washington wide receiver Gary Clark runs with the football against the Buffalo Bills in Super Bowl XXVI on January 26, 1992.

columnist Tony Kornheiser started jokingly writing about a "bandwagon" that would carry all the fans to Minneapolis, the site of that year's Super Bowl.

The bandwagon was real. So was the team. Washington steamrolled to a 14–2 record and then had little trouble in the NFC playoffs. The high-powered Buffalo Bills were the only thing standing between Washington and the championship. The Bills were in their second straight Super Bowl and had a powerful offense led by quarterback Jim Kelly and running back Thurman Thomas. Everyone was expecting a high-scoring shootout.

Washington players carry Gibbs off the field after winning Super Bowl XXVI.

Thomas, however, began the Super Bowl by losing his helmet on the sideline. It set the tone. Rypien kept working passes to Monk and Clark, while Riggs scored a pair of touchdowns to put Washington up 24–0 in the third quarter. Behind Kelly's Super Bowl-record 58 passes, the Bills attempted a late comeback. But Washington's defense tied a Super Bowl record by picking off four of them. With a 37–24 win, Washington claimed its third championship in a decade.

MOVING ON IN MORE WAYS THAN ONE

Washington made it back to the playoffs again in 1992 but lost to San Francisco in the divisional round. Two months later, Gibbs retired from coaching. Though only 52 years old, Gibbs had led the team to 140 wins and three Super Bowl titles over 12 seasons in charge. But it wasn't easy. Gibbs was known for working 100-hour weeks during the season and sleeping in his office. He hoped in retirement he could focus on his health, his family, and his other job as the owner of an auto racing team.

Washington owner Jack Kent Cooke promoted longtime defensive coordinator Richie Petitbon to take over. It didn't go well. Petitbon won his first game as head coach, a 35–16 romp over the Dallas Cowboys. It was the best moment of a miserable season. Less than 12 months after replacing Gibbs, Petitbon was fired after the team finished 4–12, the franchise's worst record in 30 years.

Cooke brought in Norv Turner in hopes of a fresh start. Turner was the offensive mastermind for the Dallas teams that won back-to-back Super Bowls in the early 1990s. Turner's time began with some of the familiar faces of Washington's glory days moving on. Monk, who had recorded his NFL-record 820th catch in 1992, left as a free agent just after Turner started. Washington let Rypien go, too.

Turner's hope was to start from scratch and mold Washington into a winner at a time when the club was moving out of RFK Stadium to a new venue in Maryland. Yet several high-profile players taken in the draft in the early 1990s never panned out. Michigan wide receiver Desmond Howard had won the 1991 Heisman Trophy

Wide receiver Art Monk left Washington after the 1993 season as the team's leader in receptions and receiving yards.

as the best player in college football. But he lasted just three years in Washington. Quarterback Heath Shuler arrived in the 1994 draft and signed the largest rookie contract in NFL history. Shuler went 4-9 as a starter before being traded to the New Orleans Saints. The team then thought it found the right quarterback in Gus Frerotte, but his time in Washington is best remembered for when he injured his neck headbutting a wall in the team's new stadium after scoring a touchdown in 1997.

A new era in the team's history began in 1999. That year, a 34-year-old businessman named Daniel Snyder led a group that purchased the team. Snyder had grown up rooting for the team and called taking over the club "a lifelong dream." He also promised to return Washington to its winning ways. The early returns were promising. Quarterback Brad Johnson and running back Stephen Davis led Washington to the NFC East title in 1999. The team then advanced to the divisional round of the playoffs before falling to the Tampa Bay Buccaneers. Nonetheless, it seemed as if the team was finally heading in the right direction.

TAKING A CHANCE

The beginning of Daniel Snyder's ownership era was highlighted by his decision to sign high-priced star players near the end of their careers, hoping they could help lead Washington back to the Super Bowl. It never happened. The list included several future Hall of Famers, including cornerback Deion Sanders and defensive end Bruce Smith. Neither reached the playoffs with Washington.

Deion Sanders

Running back Stephen Davis (48) and wide receiver Michael Westbrook (82) celebrate a Washington touchdown during the 1999 season.

However, things began to come apart during the 2000 season. The team had a winning record and was in the playoff hunt. Yet Snyder wasn't satisfied, so he fired Turner. The move began a period of instability for the team. Ahead of the 2001 campaign,

Offensive tackle Chris Samuels (60) was one of the bright spots for Washington during the 2000s, earning six Pro Bowl selections between 2001 and 2008.

Washington brought on veteran head coach Marty Schottenheimer to lead the team. He lasted just one season, during which the team went 8–8. Then Steve Spurrier, a successful college coach at Florida, came to Washington with great fanfare. After a pair of losing seasons in 2002 and 2003, Spurrier quit. Just like in the early 1980s, Washington needed a jolt. And just like in 1980, ownership turned to Joe Gibbs to provide it.

Quarterback Tim Hasselbeck couldn't lift Washington back to a winning record in 2003.

Running back Clinton Portis races away from the Tampa Bay Buccaneers for a 64-yard touchdown run in the 2004 season opener.

CHAPTER 5

AN ERA OF CHANGE

JOE GIBBS HAD BEEN RETIRED FOR 11 YEARS WHEN DANIEL SNYDER approached him about coming back to Washington. By early 2004, Gibbs had done all the things he'd set out to do when he stepped away in 1993. He'd spent time with his family. He'd focused on his health, and his stock car racing team was among NASCAR's best. It was time for a new but familiar challenge: bringing glory back to the nation's capital.

The second Gibbs era got off to a dazzling start. More than 90,000 fans showed up at what was then known as FedEx Field for the 2004 season opener. On Washington's first possession with Gibbs back on the sideline, running back Clinton Portis scored on a 64-yard sprint to the end zone. However, it proved to be one of the few highlights of a forgettable year.

Wide receiver Santana Moss caught two touchdowns in the final four minutes as Washington beat the Cowboys 14-13 in Dallas in 2005.

Washington slumped to a 6–10 record. It was the worst season of Gibbs's career at that point. The offense ranked among the league's worst, taking the shine away from a defense that was among the NFL's best. The 2005 team proved hot and cold. It ripped off five wins to close out the season and make the playoffs. The club won its playoff opener, too, before falling on the road against the Seattle Seahawks in the divisional round.

TRAGEDY AND TRIUMPH

The playoff berth was one of the highlights of Gibbs's second stint in Washington. The team slumped to a 5–11 mark in 2006 and appeared headed for another losing season in 2007. In late November, a disappointing year took a stunning and sad turn. Safety Sean Taylor, one of the best young defensive players in the league, was shot and killed in Miami when an intruder broke into his house.

Safety Sean Taylor picked off 12 passes over three-plus NFL seasons, from 2004 to 2007.

The loss of the popular Taylor devastated his teammates. The team staggered in a loss to Buffalo the week after his passing, though Portis paid tribute to his good friend in the defeat. When Portis scored a touchdown against the Bills, he raised his jersey to show fans a T-shirt featuring Taylor.

Wide receiver Antwaan Randle El scores against the Seattle Seahawks in the playoffs after the 2007 season.

Then something magical happened. A few days after Taylor's funeral, Washington went on a run. Fueled by the memory of their fallen teammate, the players reeled off wins in each of their last four games to claim a wild-card berth. However, the magic again ran out in Seattle. The Seahawks scored three touchdowns in the last seven minutes to win 35–14. Gibbs stepped away a few days later, saying he wanted to spend more time with his family.

HYPE AND HEARTBREAK

Replacing Gibbs proved to be a difficult task. Snyder spent a month interviewing coaches before settling on Jim Zorn, who had never been a high-level coach in the NFL. Zorn proved to be overmatched during two difficult years with the club. He was fired after a 4–12 season in 2009.

Snyder acted aggressively this time, bringing in former Denver Broncos head coach Mike Shanahan and paying him $7 million a season to turn the team around. Shanahan had guided the Broncos to back-to-back Super Bowls in the late 1990s behind Hall of Fame quarterback John Elway. However, there was no superstar quarterback waiting for Shanahan in Washington.

The team soon traded for Donovan McNabb, who had enjoyed several great seasons with the Philadelphia Eagles. Even though the 33-year-old quarterback got off to a slow start in 2010, Washington signed him to a huge contract in the middle of the season. However, McNabb continued to struggle, and the team traded him away the following summer.

Hope arrived in the spring of 2012. With the second pick in the draft, the team selected quarterback Robert Griffin III, who had just won the Heisman Trophy while playing for Baylor. An excellent athlete, Griffin had also been an accomplished track star during his college career. When he earned Washington's starting job out of training camp, the future again looked bright.

Washington rookie quarterback Robert Griffin III took the NFL by storm with his dual-threat abilities in 2012.

After opening the season 2–3, Washington hosted the Minnesota Vikings in Week 6. At one point, Griffin dropped back to pass before tucking the ball and racing 76 yards down the sideline for a score. His breakout moment led the team to a 38–26 victory. And the player known as "RG3" was only getting started.

Though Washington lost its next three games, the team caught fire after its Week 10 bye and closed out the season with seven straight wins. With a 10–6 record, the club won the NFC East and hosted a playoff game for the first time since the 1999 season. Griffin threw for 3,200 yards and 20 touchdowns and added 815 rushing yards and seven touchdowns on the ground on his way to winning the Rookie of the Year Award. However, he entered the playoff showdown with Seattle dealing with a sore right knee. The knee got worse against the Seahawks. He limped for most of the game and then fell while trying to recover a wayward snap, his right knee buckling in the process.

Griffin underwent surgery after the season and promised he would be ready for the start of the 2013 season. While Griffin fulfilled that promise, he was never the same. Griffin and Washington stumbled to a 3–13 mark in 2013. Shanahan was fired and replaced by Jay Gruden, who became the team's eighth different head coach during Snyder's tenure as owner.

CRADLE OF COACHES

Mike Shanahan didn't have much success leading Washington in the 2010s. But he surrounded himself with several talented young assistants. The 2013 Washington coaching staff included Mike Shanahan's son, Kyle Shanahan. Among the other assistants were Matt LaFleur, Mike McDaniel, Raheem Morris, and Sean McVay. All four went on to become head coaches, and McVay won a Super Bowl with the Los Angeles Rams.

After starting 28 games in 2012 and 2013, Griffin played in only nine more games for Washington before being released.

By the start of Gruden's second year in 2015, he decided Kirk Cousins was the best quarterback to run the offense. Cousins led Washington to an NFC East crown that season, though the team was quickly bounced out of the playoffs. Griffin was released in 2016 as a once-promising chapter in Washington came to a forgettable end.

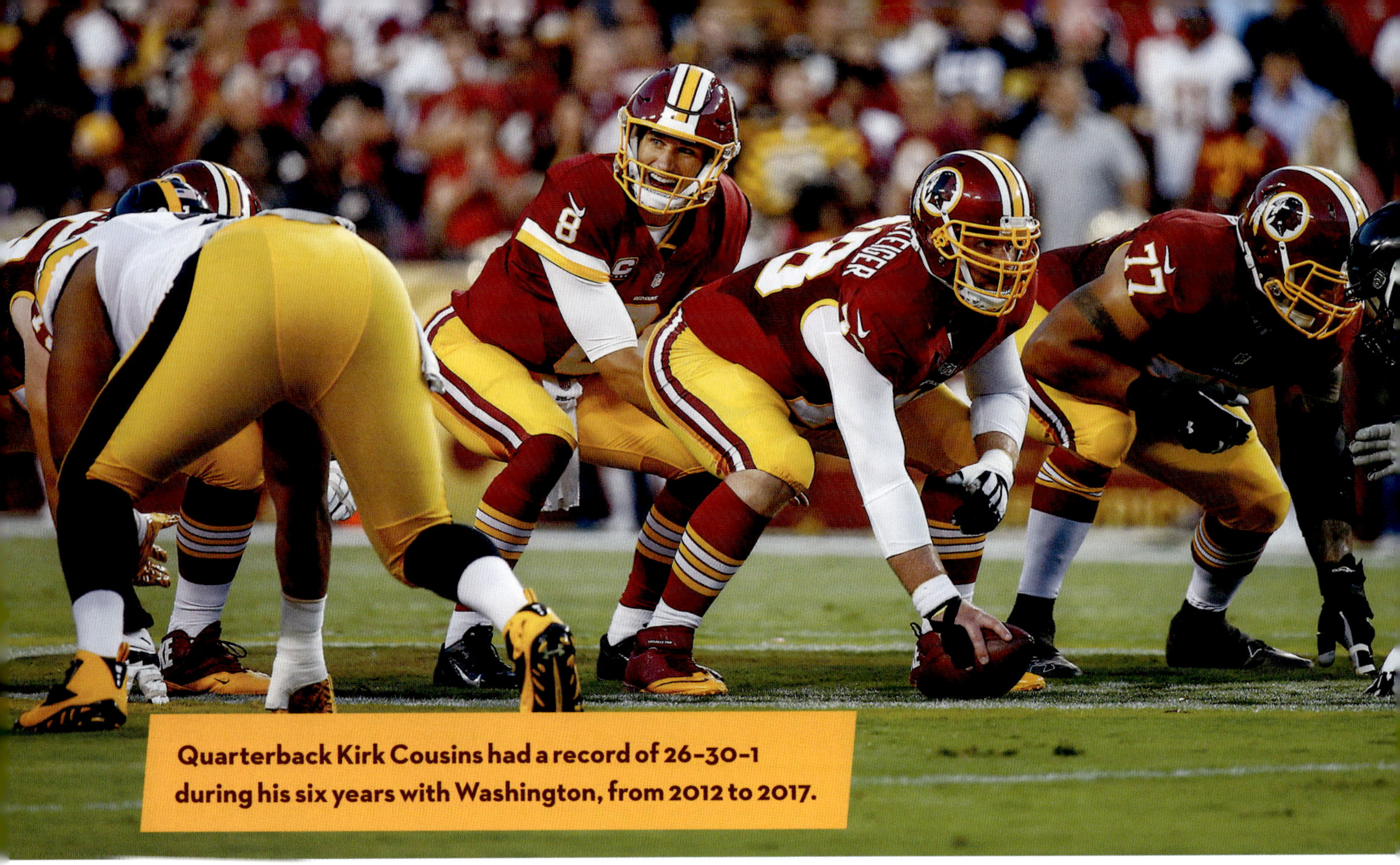

Quarterback Kirk Cousins had a record of 26-30-1 during his six years with Washington, from 2012 to 2017.

SEASONS OF CHANGE

The Gruden years were a mirror of most of the other coaching tenures of the Snyder era. Washington was occasionally competitive but rarely made a splash. The 2015 division title was the only playoff berth during Gruden's four-plus seasons. He was fired early in 2019 after Washington dropped its first five games on the way to a miserable 3-13 record.

The coaching staff wasn't the only thing changing as 2020 began. A few months after the team hired Ron Rivera as coach, the franchise retired its controversial nickname. The team had used the "Redskins" name for nearly 90 years, though it had long been considered insensitive to Native Americans. After pushing back for many years against calls to change the name and logo, the team finally accepted the change.

Commanders defensive tackle Jonathan Allen made back-to-back Pro Bowls in 2021 and 2022.

Washington did not rush to find a new nickname. It became known as the Washington Football Team for two seasons, a period that included the NFC East title in 2020 despite a 7–9 record. The club kept the team's signature burgundy-and-gold colors before selecting "Commanders" as its new nickname in February 2022.

The decision was one of Snyder's last as the team's owner. For years, he had been considered one of the worst owners in professional sports. Besides his team often struggling on the field, Snyder faced serious accusations about how he ran the club and treated its employees. After two decades in charge, he agreed to sell the team in the fall of 2022. Fans hoped the new ownership group, led by businessman Josh Harris, could bring glory back to Washington.

COMMANDERS TROPHY CASE

SUPER BOWL CHAMPIONSHIPS: 3

Super Bowl XVII – January 30, 1983
Super Bowl XXII – January 31, 1988
Super Bowl XXVI – January 26, 1992

NFL CHAMPIONSHIPS: 2

1937, 1942

CONFERENCE CHAMPIONSHIPS: 5

1972, 1982, 1983, 1987, 1991

DIVISION TITLES: 16

NFL Eastern: 1936, 1937, 1940, 1942, 1943, 1945
NFC East: 1972, 1982, 1983, 1984, 1987, 1991, 1999, 2012, 2015, 2020

All stats are through the 2024 season.

Quarterback Jayden Daniels earned the NFL's Offensive Rookie of the Year Award in 2024.

The Commanders took the first big step in that turnaround in April 2024, when they drafted quarterback Jayden Daniels. After finishing 4–13 in 2023, they improved to 12–5 in 2024. It was the team's best record since its last Super Bowl–winning season in 1991. Then Daniels led the Commanders to a pair of upset wins in the playoffs before they finally fell in the NFC title game. After three decades of disappointments, fans hoped the Commanders were finally on their way back to another championship.

TIMELINE

1932
The Boston Braves join the National Football League.

1937
Owner George Marshall moves the team, now called the Redskins, to Washington, DC. The club finishes its first season in the nation's capital by winning the NFL title.

1942
Quarterback Sammy Baugh leads Washington to its second NFL championship, a 14-6 win over the Chicago Bears.

1961
The team moves from Griffin Stadium to DC Stadium, later renamed Robert F. Kennedy Memorial Stadium.

1973
George Allen's "Over the Hill Gang" reaches the Super Bowl, but Washington falls 14-7 to the Miami Dolphins on January 14.

1983
Washington finishes off a season interrupted by a players' strike by defeating Miami 27-17 in the Super Bowl. John Riggins is the MVP after running for a Super Bowl-record 166 yards and the clinching touchdown.

1984
Washington sets an NFL record for points (541) during the 1983 season but is upset by the Los Angeles Raiders 38-9 in the Super Bowl.

1988
Doug Williams throws four touchdown passes during a 35-point outburst in the second quarter as Washington beats Denver 42-10 to win its second Super Bowl.

1992
Washington claims its third Super Bowl in 10 years, beating the Buffalo Bills 37-24 behind an MVP performance by quarterback Mark Rypien.

1996
Washington plays its final game at RFK Stadium, a 37-10 win over the Dallas Cowboys. The team moves into Jack Kent Cooke Stadium in Landover, Maryland, in 1997.

2020
The franchise retires its longtime nickname. After going as the Washington Football Team for two seasons, the team becomes the Washington Commanders in 2022.

2024
Rookie quarterback Jayden Daniels leads the Commanders to a 12-5 record and eventually the NFC title game.

GLOSSARY

blitz—when a linebacker or defensive back attacks the line of scrimmage to stop a run or sack the quarterback.

contract—an agreement to play for a certain team.

coordinator—an assistant coach who is in charge of the offense, defense, or special teams.

draft—a system that allows teams to acquire new players coming into the league.

dynasty—a team that has an extended period of success, usually winning multiple championships in the process.

found—to establish something.

franchise—an entire sports organization.

free agent—a player who is not signed to a team.

general manager—an executive who runs a team and is responsible for finding and signing players.

integrate—bring people who had been discriminated against into an institution.

retire—to end one's career.

rival—an opponent with whom a player or team has a fierce and ongoing competition.

rookie—a professional athlete in his or her first year of competition.

sack—a tackle of the quarterback behind the line of scrimmage before he can pass the ball.

slur—an insulting or belittling word or phrase.

strike—refusing to work as a form of protest, usually about things such as working conditions and wages.

tenure—a period of time in which somebody holds a position.

upset—an unexpected victory by a supposedly weaker team or player.

versatile—able to perform many different roles or functions.

veteran—someone who has played for many years.

wild-card—the first round of the playoffs.

ONLINE RESOURCES

Booklinks
NONFICTION NETWORK
FREE! ONLINE NONFICTION RESOURCES

To learn more about the Washington Commanders, please visit **abdobooklinks.com** or scan this QR code. These links are routinely monitored and updated to provide the most current information available.

INDEX